7/10 25.65

D1212291

Molly
Pitcher

A Buddy Book
by
Christy DeVillier

ABDO
Publishing Company

VISIT US AT

www.abdopub.com

Published by ABDO Publishing Company, 4940 Viking Drive, Suite 622, Edina, Minnesota 55435. Copyright © 2004 by Abdo Consulting Group, Inc. International copyrights reserved in all countries. No part of this book may be reproduced in any form without written permission from the publisher.

Printed in the United States.

Edited by: Michael P. Goecke
Contributing Editor: Matt Ray
Image Research: Deborah Coldiron
Graphic Design: Jane Halbert
Cover Photograph: Library of Congress
Interior Photographs/Illustrations: Hulton Archives, Library of Congress, North Wind, Photodisc

Library of Congress Cataloging-in-Publication Data

DeVillier, Christy, 1971–
     Molly Pitcher / Christy DeVillier.
        v. cm. — (First biographies)
     Includes index.
     Contents: Who is Molly Pitcher?—Molly's true name—Moving Away—Joining the Revolution—Valley Forge—Battle of Monmouth—Rewarding Molly.
     ISBN 1-59197-515-8
     1. Pitcher, Molly, 1754–1832—Juvenile literature. 2. Monmouth, Battle of, Freehold, N.J., 1778—Juvenile literature. 3. Women revolutionaries—United States—Biography—Juvenile literature. 4. United States—History—Revolution, 1775–1783—Women—Juvenile literature. 5. United States—History—Revolution, 1775–1783—Biography—Juvenile literature. [1. Pitcher, Molly, 1754–1832. 2. Monmouth, Battle of, Freehold, N.J., 1778. 3. United States—History—Revolution, 1775–1783—Biography. 4. Women—Biography.] I. Title.

E241.M7D48 2004
973.3'34'092—dc21
[B]
                                                                      2003052260

Table Of Contents

5887913

Who Is Molly Pitcher?

Molly Pitcher is an American hero. She fought in a famous battle in the Revolutionary War. People remember Molly Pitcher for her bravery.

Molly Pitcher is a Revolutionary War hero.

Molly's Real Name

Molly Pitcher was born around 1754. But Molly was not her real name. Her parents named her Mary.

Mary and her family lived in Pennsylvania. At that time, Pennsylvania was a British colony. Mary and her family were colonists. They lived under British law.

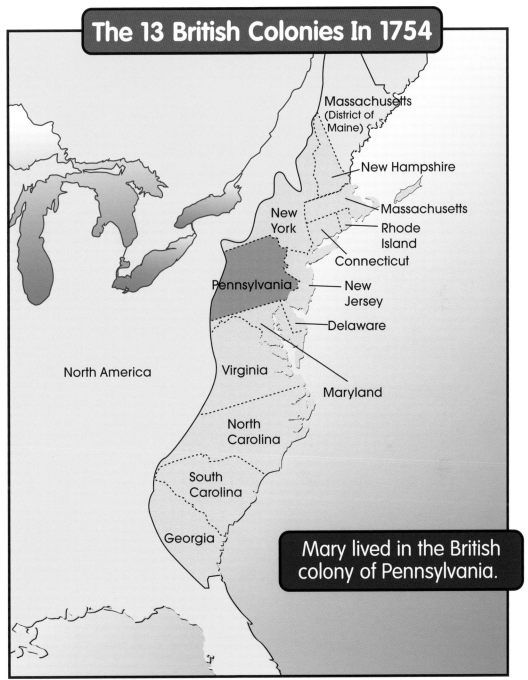

The 13 British Colonies In 1754

Massachusetts
(District of
Maine)

New Hampshire

New
York

Massachusetts

Rhode
Island

Connecticut

Pennsylvania

New
Jersey

Delaware

North America

Virginia

Maryland

North
Carolina

South
Carolina

Georgia

Mary lived in the British colony of Pennsylvania.

Moving Away

Mary grew up near Philadelphia, Pennsylvania. She moved to Carlisle, Pennsylvania, around 1769. She worked as a maid for Dr. William Irvine.

Mary married a barber in Carlisle. A barber cuts men's hair. His name was William Hays.

A barber cuts hair for men and boys.

Joining The Revolution

Over time, many colonists became unhappy with Britain. They complained about British taxes. Some colonists wanted to be free of British rule. They wanted to form their own country.

Colonists dumped British tea to protest a new tea tax.

In 1775, a battle broke out between British troops and colonists. This was the beginning of the Revolutionary War. The colonies began fighting for their freedom.

William Hays joined the Continental army in 1775. He became an American soldier.

Mary traveled with her husband and the army. She cooked, cleaned, and mended clothes. Mary did a lot to help William and the other soldiers.

This is what a soldier from the Continental army looked like.

Revolutionary Women

   Colonists who supported the American Revolution were called Patriots. Many Patriots joined the Continental army.

   Women were not allowed in the army back then. So, women Patriots did other important things. Some Patriot women sewed shirts for American soldiers. Others spied on British troops.

Catherine Schuyler was a Patriot.

One famous Patriot was Catherine Schuyler. Her husband was a general in the Continental army. She looked after their farm when he was away. A famous painting shows Catherine preparing for British soldiers. She is burning her fields so they cannot eat her crops.

Valley Forge

George Washington was the leader of the Continental army. He led the Continental army to Valley Forge, Pennsylvania, in 1777. Mary and William marched with them. They spent the cold winter there.

American soldiers spent the winter of 1777 and 1778 in Valley Forge, Pennsylvania.

The winter at Valley Forge was a bad time for American soldiers. They did not have enough food or warm clothes. Many soldiers died.

In the spring, American soldiers began training again. They learned a lot from a Prussian soldier. His name was Baron von Steuben. With his help, the Continental army became better soldiers.

Baron von Steuben

Battle Of Monmouth

The Battle of Monmouth broke out on June 28, 1778. Mary and her husband were there. William was a gunner. He worked at a cannon.

Cannons were an important part of Revolutionary War battles.

This battle happened on a hot summer day. The soldiers became hot and thirsty. So, Mary grabbed her pitcher and filled it with water. She braved bullets to bring water to the soldiers. This is how Mary got the name "Molly Pitcher."

General George Washington led soldiers at the Battle of Monmouth.

During the battle, Mary's husband became weak from the heat. He could not work the cannon. So, Mary took his place on the battlefield. This was a dangerous job. But Mary braved the enemy's fire. She kept working at the cannon.

Mary bravely worked at a cannon during the Battle of Monmouth.

Rewarding Mary

The state of Pennsylvania gave Mary a pension for her war service. Some people say George Washington heard of Mary's bravery. He may have made her a sergeant.

George Washington became the
first president of the United States.

Mary died in 1832. But Americans have not forgotten her bravery. Today, they call Molly Pitcher an American hero.

Mary was buried in Carlisle, Pennsylvania. A statue stands by her grave. A cannon is there, too. It reminds Americans of Mary's bravery on the battlefield.

The statue of Molly Pitcher at her grave in Carlisle, Pennsylvania.

Another Molly Pitcher

Margaret Corbin was another brave woman of the American Revolution. People called Margaret "Molly Pitcher," too. Like Mary, Margaret brought water to soldiers on the battlefield.

Margaret's husband died in battle on November 16, 1776. Margaret took over for him at the cannon. She fired the cannon until she was shot in the shoulder.

Important Dates

1754 Mary, or "Molly Pitcher," is born around this time.

1769 Mary begins working for Dr. William Irvine.

1775 The Revolutionary War begins. Mary's husband joins the Continental army.

July 4, 1776 American leaders sign the Declaration of Independence.

Winter 1777–1778 Mary and William spend a cold winter in Valley Forge, Pennsylvania.

June 28, 1778 The Battle of Monmouth takes place. Mary takes over for her husband on the battlefield.

October 19, 1781 America wins the Revolutionary War.

1822 The state of Pennsylvania rewards Mary with a pension.

1832 Mary dies. She is buried in Carlisle, Pennsylvania.

Important Words

colony a settlement. Colonists are the people who live in a colony.

Patriot the name for colonists who believed in the American Revolution.

pension money given as a reward in return for war service.

Revolutionary War the war Americans fought to win their freedom from Britain.

spy to secretly watch what others are doing.

tax money charged by a city or country.

Web Sites

To learn more about Molly Pitcher, visit ABDO Publishing Company on the World Wide Web at www.abdopub.com. Web sites about Molly Pitcher are featured on our Book Links page. These links are routinely monitored and updated to provide the most current information available.

Index